The
Moon
Rises
with
Light

JAMES TAKYI

ISBN paperback 978-1-7358276-0-5
ISBN hardcover 978-1-7358276-1-2
ISBN ebook 978-1-7358276-2-9

ACKNOWLEDGEMENTS

I want to express thanks to my mother for the gift of life, sacrifice, nurturing, and care—for constantly encouraging me to reach beyond my horizon.

"All that I am or hope to be, I owe to my angel mother."
—Abraham Lincoln

To Jade, my partner, my wife, my best friend who teaches me every day how to tend to the garden of love.

"A true partner or friend is one who encourages
you to look deep inside yourself for the beauty
and love you've been seeking."
—Thích Nhất Hạnh

To you—children, Makaya and CJ who teach me patience, humility—helping me to find glee in your innocence. To Makaya for naming the book.

"The most precious inheritance that parents can
give their children is their own happiness."
—Thích Nhất Hạnh

You who helped mold me.
You who have supported and been beside me
through the hills and valleys.

To family and friends:
Thank you for your support, encouragement,
and feedback all hours of the day and night.
From brainstorming book cover designs to editing
and coming up with a title—I feel the love,
and for that I am grateful.

"I am grateful to have been loved
and to be loved now and to be able to love,
because love liberates.
Love liberates, it doesn't just hold,
that's ego, love liberates!"
–Maya Angelou

In addition, I am grateful and fortunate to
Editor Eric Muhr and Designer Asya Blue—thank you
so much for your expertise and commitment
to help me see this through.

———————————————

CONTENTS

The Awakening 1

When It Falls 35

Overcome. 56

Seeing and Knowing 66

Breath. 75

Love 84

Fire 95

Amun 112

THE AWAKENING

In the depth of despair
have hope.
In the silence of the night,
keep your dreams alive.
With the awakening of the sun,
let fears fade with ablutions.

———————————————

I TOO AM AMERICAN

I too am American—
man, woman, human;
I am no venomous serpent
whereby keeping neck bound keeps you safe.
How large is your frustration to carry hate so great?
A veil of ignorance so thick
you want to beat me with a stick,
shoot me with a gun,
insult with a pun,
enslave, shun, oppress, suppress.
What a heavy conflict to carry,
to know that
no matter what you do,
you still see your humanness in me.
Is that why you are angry?
You don't want to let the truth be.

To know that this mind,
our minds, speaks and articulates,
strives and achieves,
greatness, beauty—
while some falling prey to similar ignorance,
identical hate—because the truth is,
we are not so different.
We are the interwoven tapestry—
variety of humanity— all together earthling.
Truth is truth whether you acknowledge it or not.
To embrace it is freedom. Cut the cables of labels:
Freedom to love and to care, to connect, grow and share,
to shed the mirage of fear,
to have the depth of satisfaction that liberates hair,
blood, bones to mind.
Be happy, be peaceful, be liberated.

———————————————————

BREAKING CHAINS

The links of time
interlock their cold, lifeless curves from Mom and Dad,
son and daughter,
sister, brother, uncle, aunt—
recreating toxic wounds and normalized extremes.
Even after the hurt,
the mind holds on to the pain—
in a pause—
talking opens old wounds,
so we turn away,
masking vulnerabilities with defenses,
absences, and gaps of recollection,

mines ready to explode with the smell of a scent,
a sound, a taste, or feeling on the skin.
Survivors walking with frozen memories,
internalized enemies.
Life goes on; every tomorrow melts or hardens the frost.
Some take this jumping, kicking bull of fear by the horns
and ride it into submission—ride into exhaustion,
knowing very well that this road is unpredictable,
rugged, ever-changing.
This ride demands a tight grip,
honesty, acceptance, determination, persistence,
concentration, perseverance,
and more importantly,
kindness for ourselves.

_____

COLOR BLIND

Do you think your existence is more important than mine?
When you use words of hate to define my race,
where culture and color are mixed,
nothing truly different exists,
and still
your hate persists,
yet you wonder why I raise my fist.
Your words sting, and I cry, but I don't wish you to die.
I laugh as you try to pry hate from inside
because you find at the bottom of this depth
is where love truly lies,
inside no disguise.
Besides, it's time for our differences to subside
and for you to see me as someone alive.

BULLY

My sanity
is not lacking without your psychopathic influence.
Picture yourself in my place, in my shoes,
and if you can't, allow me to inflict some pain on you.
But I won't.
So the abuse continues.
Monday: faggot. Tuesday: whore, queer.
Queer, that's what you are, right? Asked the tyrant. Right?
Subdued and bewildered, I nodded in agreement.
Oh Friday, why are you so far away?
Minutes feel like hours.
Rather than fight back against the enemy,
the fight is within me.
They are sharks, and my blood is aromatic.
At home, the torture plays over and over in my head.
My heart pounds faster and harder
with every thought of the abuse.
I am afraid.

The anticipation of the next day promotes anxiety
that causes me to be unable to sleep.
The walk to the bus stop weighs on me
as if I carry a crucifix on my back.
Each bus ride is a trip into the womb of doom
the birthplace of terror where I am to be oppressed.
Then the arrival
marks the beginning of my walk into Hades, where the
beast lies.
The dragon and its demons,
thirsting and aching to eat my flesh and salt my wounds.
Each day feels like an eternity.
It is exhausting. I want it to end.
It will end.

———————

WARRIOR EYES

I chose to be a weapon,
but they made me what I am.
I chose to shoot strangers to protect strangers.
I chose not to ask questions. Just do it and try to forget it.
I feel love and compassion fading with every breath
yet still struggling to survive within my heart.
When I was a civilian, I felt I had no purpose—
just some foolish boy with dreams bound to fail.
I was a misfit, a girl with no future—
misunderstood and abused, shunned and accused.
So my anger became my sanity,
thinking war was what I saw in fantasy.
So I became one in many armies, molded with discipline.
Then there is the real deal.
Whistling bullets and explosions, aiming to end my life—
our lives.
The only cause out there is survival.
There is no turning back. Either they die, or we die—

desensitized—
and now they are no longer human in my eyes.
I am convinced to call it the devil. I allowed him.
It was foolish.
Now I have what I wanted. I have purpose.
I kill.
I am seen as the grim reaper in some neighborhoods.
What a sad story, some might say,
but who says, I am crying.
Sad is not a word I even consider.
I am a warrior.
All I wanted was escape from home.
How did I end up here?

———————————

HALO

Life is green,
beautiful scenes that connect to a beautiful sky
until the devil takes a bite of your flesh.
He craves for more and more.
The climax is when you take your last breath.
She takes your whole heart and cuts it into separate parts,
plucking your eyes out just to get to your brain.
So now back to that beautiful scene, green,
where the river flows in between mountains with icy tops.
Daffodils and rainbows
are the mind hallucinating the pain away,
and with the revolution of the hour hand
around coefficients,
you teleported from your spaceship into Hades.
The fire within flesh seems to be everlasting,
loathing the existence of life. You flash back, and you're
there,
walking down the red brick road with your M16
as the wizard taunts you,

reminding you that he owns you.
Now your dark clouds separate, creating an opening.
Light shines through, dominating the darkness.
Now your fears are but shadows.
The road ahead seems bright,
as long as this light keeps shining.

—————————————————————

LOSS

Please, please say it ain't so.
Tears sprint out of my eyes and swim down my cheeks.
Say it ain't so.
She was my best friend; he was my brother;
she—my mother, my sister.
So this is my reality.
I pinch myself to escape and awake from this darkness.
I am screaming inside, but no one hears my voice.
Memories have become my enemy,
so I get angry at GOD and everyone around me.
I beg, and I cry—suddenly I believe in miracles.
I wait impatiently for mine, for a sign.
This helpless emotion is my new addiction.
This pain has injured my feeble body—
the magnitude, the burden—
cursing at the heavens
as the weight forces me down on my knees.
My sunshine is gloom.

My heart only sees doom.
One tip of this glass
and the grim sight of lifeless flesh in a tomb—
life has wounded my heart.
Life has scrambled my sanity.
The wind has blown the fire from this melting candle.
I Will Rest. In. Peace.

THE JOURNEY

Lost in a fog, I am taught to hold on,
to defy gravity, rise above poverty, and be
what I want to be.
This is what my mother has taught me.
This is what the world has shown me.
So I chase my dreams and bring to fruition what was
hoped, and rise.
I shall fall in the dust, yet it is not my time to live in it,
so up I go, standing and walking, heart swelling with fear
that gradually subsides.
I shall surprise hateful eyes.
I shall shine like a star in the sky.
I rise to a land of opportunity, the land of milk and honey.
So is my story
our journey.
Amen.

_____

THE SKY IS FALLING

Crash!
Ash like snowflakes from heaven
bringing all the baggage the devil left behind.
Crash!
False prophets with hidden agendas
brainwashing your eye sockets to kill,
putting people's lives in danger.
Now misfortune has the dark forces writing history.
Two times five is ten, said the teacher as my paper listened
to my pen—
as bodies fell from the sky while a country was terrorized—
as two towers fell,
I saw the true capacity of man that turned the earth into hell.

RUN ON

Histories clasp, tell stories of the past crash or triumphant
man's ways of past days now history crusades bloody
battles and joyful victory parades of the warriors' weapons
of choice steel that will silence a voice or voices shouting
freedom priests kill the bloody heathen's imams behead
the infidel hell's presence felt now but they say it's a world
away the king had a dream found shattered on a balcony
wall but bullet fragments only killed the man with blood
red like any other I got down on my knees and wrote a
letter to God then Amun-Ra sealed and sent it first-class
mail Germans shouting heil hitler kill the Jews they deserve
a bruise or two cool brainwashing cold steel piercing
frostbitten feet ashes of young and old like you and me free
freedom has been won blood has been shed tears escape
the emotions out of eye sockets fled.

THE POWER OF LOVE

Let oceans sing as voices cry,
and don't forget, let freedom reign.
Times get tough, yet we will defy,
and don't forget, let freedom reign.
Trials and tribulation,
joys and jubilation,
wars of all these nations,
blood as life is taken.
Death does not silence civil unrest,
so we rest, and we sit as we are punched and kicked
with fists in the sky
because we don't just live to die.
We live to love and to cry.
We live for the good days and good nights,
the hellos and goodbyes,

fall only to spread our wings and fly.
We live to survive seemingly endless dark skies
because when oppressed, people will defy.
People will defy hatred
as they are deceived into poison gas chambers
or tortured for the sake of sport.
People will defy oppression
as they are kidnapped
and transported in their own feces and urine
to face eternal slavery.
People have defied genocide—
count-less injustice—the limit is the sky, yet we survive.

THE AFRICAN SLAVE

The journey felt long and endless,
and now it seems
we are no longer on the devil's road.
We are in its lair.
Somehow I still have a bit of dignity left,
flowing through crying veins
hidden beneath battered flesh,
and with that, I stand tall.
Even as they humiliate me, I stand tall.
The cold, hard, unforgiving chains
around our necks and wrists bring tears
to the eyes of the strongest amongst us
as we walk miles to the gates of no return.
This evil is like none I have ever seen.
After many mornings
of humiliation and torture,
many nights
enduring screams of rape,
the sight of abuse after abuse
and scent of death,

they gathered enough of us
to satisfy their greed.
After many nights and days of horror,
they gathered enough of us
to pack on wretched ships.
They had heard enough screams
and had seen enough blood
to satisfy their savage thirst.
Elmina, the devils' fortress,
was only the beginning of the journey.

FREEDOM LAND

Selma, Alabama,
1965.
A bright, sunny, summer, Sunday morning,
and in the distance was this,
"Ain't gonna let nobody turn me around,
 turn me around."
They kept moving forward
regardless of known terrors that were ahead—
the vicious dogs,
the fire hoses and violent men with clubs.
Envious of their courage,
watching from behind the windowsill,
humbled,
I wanted to tell them that
not all of us are ignorant, misguided, and full of hate.
I stood there, fixed with unwavering eyes,
moved by their determination.

They were many.
Marching rebels,
walking side by side with interlocked arms,
soon they were out of view, but
I could still hear their chanting,
repeating their declaration
over and over, tirelessly.
"Ain't gonna let nobody turn me around,
marching on to freedom land."
Words that I find myself reciting silently
under my breath
whenever life knocks me down.

———————————————

DRIVE-BY

To my right
the drunk man,
stumbling with every step,
drowning in his own sadness,
swimming in absence of self and sanity.
The drunk man,
walking below the orange, glowing streetlight
as we drive by.
Each step he takes is a new direction.
He hugs the wall as he nearly falls—
each step is a near-death experience.
What a fool, I think,
as I question my confused sympathy,
ignorant to his joy,
oblivious to his pain.
Is his aim to forget
or to accept the circumstances of life?
So now I am at a red light—
even more reason to stare
and contemplate the ambiguous view.

IN THE BLINK OF AN EYE

Intoxicated in the day,
darkness falls in the eyes of the drunk like it's late,
life taken away. I pray
for the dead whose blood on the ground spreads,
blood splatters and bones not broken but shattered,
as if life on a falling platter—
voices scream in agony—
the one who loved life
and the other lost in depression and death caressing.
The scope of hope now narrowed
Awakening to the bitterness of tomorrow
Eyes wet with tears
Heartbroken with shame
the depth of regret
while fingers point the blame.
Who is there to really blame?

_____

INCOMPLETE

I'm looking for a way to not be broken,
to be reawakened,
trying to find the courage to not be sad,
a way to accept the bad.
I need a song to sing my emotions,
to help me forget why I'm so hurt.
I need an escape to make me happy,
one that doesn't bring old feelings back.
I don't want to be afraid of the silence,
these thoughts that haunt me.
Giving all that I have to this bottomless pit
as life cracks its punishing whip.
Constructing and reconstructing the past,
I'm tired of being sick, chasing a mirage,
going through the motions
but mentally parked in my garage,
processing garbage.
Pushing and pulling experiences that never last,
the future is my present, but I'm presently out of gas.

JUDAS

Mr. Pastor, this is my last dollar.
I am desperate for money
because my children need to eat.
Mr. Pastor,
ain't nothing cooking above the fire,
my children are hungry, and they can't sleep.
Their papa is in heaven now—
why Mr. Pastor does God not answer me?
I am poor as can be,
Mr. Pastor, why me? why me?
Mr. Pastor,
you took my dollar and didn't seem to care
that I am still standing here
waiting for God to answer my prayer.
Pastor Jones,
your children are warm at home,
and my children are in the cold.
Do you think this is fair?
Pastor Jones,
you helped me believe that Jesus is only here,
only to realize that Jesus is everywhere.
Judas Jones, heart of stone,
here I am—

flesh, blood, and bones
in what you claim to be God's home.
Judas, you spat lies in my face
and made me feel guilty so I would stay.
Now, old and gray, and you are still the same way.
My children are better off today,
but I will never forget the lesson of how Judas betrayed.

PUBLIC ENEMY

I am a public enemy.
Police come to my home
with guns and knives trying to silence me,
but I won't stop the rioting.
I won't stop telling the truth
about what you done to me.
You brought me straight out of Africa,
where I had the update on technology
like architecture,
but nevertheless,
you still dragged me in chains to America,
land of the free—
beat me,
raped me,
made me a slave
and made me call you master.
You have created a monster, an enemy,
and you must pay the price
for the actions of cruelty you inflicted on me.

Martin Luther King Jr. had a dream,
and through me it will be seen.
I will not fail. I will succeed and
let the name of the black race be redeemed.
I don't have any bad intentions.
I'm just trying to give people a real connection
of what's been bottled up inside my people
for many generations—
we are tired of white oppression,
daily tax collection,
health care rejection and
making us seem like we are not part
of this nation.
People turn away from truth today.
They want to live in fantasy and fiction
because to them, reality is not appealing.
This life has robbed me of my dignity,
now I face a death penalty,
and who wants to hear the words of a public enemy?

TRIBAL BOY

I am a tribal boy,
obeying constitutional laws,
living in a country that sells itself
like an item in a store,
not caring about its children,
injuring them with war.
Every day I step out my door
I feel like I am on a battle front.
Jehovah's Witnesses
go by preaching the word of the Lord,
but are only denied with slammed doors
of parents who can't control their children,
who end up drinking and thinking
it will alleviate their problems and bad feelings.
I have the freedom of speech,
that's what they teach,
but when they see my outreach
they turn their backs on me
and let me burn in hell—
when they see success and money,
to me their products they want to sell.
I'm in a state of poverty
living in the projects with no money.

I want to liberate my mind from this cage.
Till this day I still do the time
for a crime I didn't commit.
Lawyers want money
so the truth they will submit,
without that they don't want to hear it.
There are hard working parents
who leave kids unattended,
thinking they can care for themselves,
but their minds ain't grown,
they are just kids with hormones
who might end up doing drugs,
when all they need is someone to care,
someone to give them hugs.
Some kids have parents
who wake up at the crack of dawn
and work outrageous shifts
just to get some cold hard cash
while their children are going bad
selling crack on lawns and
failing every high school class.
But I am a tribal boy.
What do I know?

———————————

I HAVE A DREAM

This is a time
for we, the American people
to exercise our right
to demand an honest government.
We are of all nations and different backgrounds
together on one land because we have dreams.
Dreams of freedom, opportunity, success.
Well, my fellow Americans,
it is time.
Don't sit around staring at passing clouds
and let your dreams pass you by.
It is time for change, and the time is now!
Our dreams of peace
have been ripped from us, time and time again.
How much more will we take
before we realize
that we have the power to change ourselves,
to influence others and the world?

Don't bow your heads in regret
for past mistakes,
but rather learn from them
and lift your heads high,
but don't forget honor.
We are a strong nation
but a nation divided
soon to unite.
Soon to see the light beyond these dark times
that surround us with constant carnage.
Soon to repair this global damage.
It starts with a dream.

———————————

WHEN IT FALLS

Happiness is not an accident.
It takes work.
It's cultivated.
If we wake up in the morning and don't practice
observation of our thoughts and actions,
if we don't eat food
that allows body to work properly
and don't listen to music
that plants loving seeds in the mind,
if we don't prepare the soil
and nurture crops of peace,
of love and happiness in ourselves,
then we are not going to embody happiness.
Be happy my friends.

MIRAGE

Have you ever wondered
if another woman has been in your bed?
The thought that keeps you up like a thorn in your head.
This idea that causes distance between you and your man,
Saying, "I love you," with resistance in your tongue.
The thought that makes you so angry
it stops air from entering your lungs.
Is she in my bed now?
You ask yourself as the workday goes by.
Is she taking a bite out of the apple of my eye?
Trying to play detective
but find no trace of the phantom whore,
paranoid you gather all the evidence you think you find,
but nothing adds up, so it seems you are losing your mind.
Crumbling under the weight,
you find every excuse to hold him tight,
but every second together seems to lead to a fight.
Now it's come to this, hiding behind your own fence,
watching, hoping he was honest in his defense.

Waiting and waiting for hours,
patiently praying that you are wrong.
But as the clock struck 12,
the truth is revealed.
Standing outside your window,
you watch her take the last bite—
falling to the ground, you have nothing left in you to fight.
The seeds of hope fall hopelessly to the ground,
so is the end when it all falls down.

———————————————

DARK

You hateful pile of filth.
You disgust me,
stabbing and stabbing and stabbing with your words.
Wounds deeper than oil wells,
pain masked with a smile—you vile dog of a man.
Rolling my life around as if a game of dice.
You bastard!
You will get a taste of your own bitter medicine.
I will be at the receiving end of your blows no more.
No more shall I be your victim.
I will be no one's victim,
no man's victim.
Never.
Love's bitter taste has taken refuge in my heart.
I will fear no more.
You will burn, and I will spit on your ashes,
make a fortress of your bones,
and make it known that I am a victim no more.

Thank you for the gift of rage.
Thank you for the scars and broken bones,
the concussions and depression
because now,
it is all on you.
After all,
it is you who made me realize
I have nothing to lose.

————————————

MISLED

Can't fight this feeling that is coming over me,
the glance from across the room,
undressing me—
who does that man want me to be,
provoking mystery casually—
a mistress, a maid,
or maybe a queen?
It is interesting how he can't seem to see
that I am a married woman,
committed as can be,
but I will allow him to dream a young
man's fantasy
and plant a seductive seed.
I will allow him to take it all in—
the bouncing hair, the rolling lips,
the curvy hips, skin soft and fair.
Then he stands and confidently moves my way,
unsuspecting that today just isn't his day.

The closer he gets, the more nervous I become:
what have I done?
He leans against the bar and faces me,
calling with a stern yet subtle voice,
"Excuse me?"
With a smile rising on my face, I turn.
Repeating his words again,
"Excuse me?!
Two drinks
for the ladies at the table in the corner."

BRAIN SCATTER

I want to sail the curves of her ocean
and dive into the depth of her heart.
I want to capture every moment—prolong—
but the fragrance of this flower is temporary.
Free me from this belligerent evil.
Ghosts escape my throat,
striking fear in your soul.
Do you seek my demise?
For at times, it is you I despise.
Don't cry butterfly.
Preying on my weakness,
you smell regret in my sighs.
You defuse the anger in my bloodshot eyes,
so I fall for the bait—
I drop the weight of bewildering hate,
and there,
you escape the terror which was to be your fate.
Oh, this beautiful butterfly.

My eyes are fixed on her as she floats to the sky,
her array of colors has my eyes hypnotized.
I want to sail the curves of her ocean
and dive into the depth of her heart.
I want to capture every moment—prolong—
but her sweetness is poison
slithering her venom into my veins, and my mind bemuse
Rescue me—
I am her puppet.
She pulls my strings to entertain her depression.
She reads me like a book
as I flip through page after page without escape—
my sanity is now a mere internal debate.

———————————————————

UNFAITHFUL

My heart is drowning.
Many lives have suffered more severe atrocities,
yet heartbreak is agonizing, nonetheless.
You see, what makes it so painful is that
you took it all away from me.
The bold, wet, gleaming eyes that saw me,
those which convinced me without an utter of sound
that I am secure with you.
You loved her with those hands which have known me,
those which comforted me,
those which have journeyed and discovered
the sands of my soul.
You used to excite me like a child with sweets.
I enjoyed the spontaneous ways you crept into my mind
unannounced—
the pleasure of seeing you
would make my heart skip a beat.
I am suffocating.
Oh, you gave it all away.

Your lips joined with hers
and wrestled for the attention of a lover,
pushing and pulling,
softly convincing them that hers are better than mine.
The invisible solidarity, which was us has died.
That is why I mourn, for we shall never be.
You have become nothing but a wound in my chest.
I will not dwell in sorrow for with every tomorrow
my wounds heal.
My scars shall tell the tale of my pain.
This is my burden to bear.
So what do you have to say, standing there
with your foolish glare,
gazing at me with your shameful stare,
as if I am a vicious bear?
Do you even care?

———————————

PURPLE DRESS FEELING BLUE

Her eyes met mine, and there it was,
a sign of vulnerability that said, hold me.
Her lips uttered words that echoed her desire.
She exhaled all her fears and woes,
and it poured and poured until it was time for class.
So we said our goodbyes, but
as the clicking and clacking of her shoes grew distant,
I felt compelled to pursue her—
I hurried with the quickness of a cheetah with
the wind on my side,
and when I arrived,
she smiled
as though her prayers were answered.
We walked and talked some more.
I felt a connection to this woman.
Her frustration and anguish became mine.
If only life were a fairy tale,
where I could sweep this beauty off her feet
and save the day.

We reached the end of the road,
but it seemed
this was just the beginning of something new.
So as the quest and signals of the end
became apparent,
she slowly inched forward.
I knew the moment was right.
I pulled her close,
wrapped my arms around her body, and there it was.
It was not lust nor love but rather a feeling of joy—
a comfort, a feeling of hope that everything will be okay.

FALLEN

Falling from the heaven in his eyes,
truth revealed from the broken seal,
troubled past is history,
it doesn't make me.
Growth out of the battle,
the poor, negative, statistical cycle,
holy angel over my shoulder
still not committed to the Bible.
Imperfection is human—perfection is God's.
This is the resurrection,
mental reconstruction.
Ignorance is bliss, so I chose the path less traveled by.
Honesty never needs an alibi.
Standing tall, righteous, and intellectual,
this is reality, mind, body, and spiritual—
I abide by an oath to be better.
Never seize to grow.
Tomorrow and tomorrow and tomorrow,

falling from the heaven in his eyes,
where my sunshine fades away, and blue skies turn gray—
lost in the stampede of strife,
floating like a feather through spontaneous skies,
driving on this uncertain road called life,
soaring through its storms,
navigating its turns, learning to read the signs.

BREAK UP

The wait is getting more and more difficult as time goes by.
The days crawl,
like an earthworm
painfully inching my emotions along.
The nights get harder.
I catch myself breathless, restless, feeling helpless—
I cannot imagine life without her.
She is the air I breathe, and I—am—suffocating.
My heart just wants to give up.
At times I feel so lost—
lost in the depth of true love denied, true love intensified.
I ask myself sometimes if waiting is the right thing to do,
or should I call my love?
I pray, and I'm told to be patient, prepared.
This love intensified has left me weak,
pretending to be alive.
I hate this feeling of constant hunger.
I am afraid to admit that it has defeated my strength.
But I wait.
This feeling divine—this feeling in my voice, in my heart,
and in every part of my being.
Abundant in its ways, I serve.
I am a student of love.

LOST MY MIND TEMPORARILY

You slit my throat slowly with a dull blade,
but I feel the sharpness of it.
My blood splatters, burning your eyes
until teardrops fall from red clouds.
This feeling is overbearing—
strangers walk by, laughing at my struggle to shout.
I can feel their eyes sting as if waiting to feed,
itching to pounce, as I bleed.
The smell of blood fills the air, and they can taste it.
My honor is stable, but my pride is weak,
and now, my head
without a body
stands at the edge of a spear.

THE END

Over time I have become
the pacifier to your soulful, woeful cries.
I am the grass that softens the collisions of your step
against the earth.
This was not the role I signed up for in this
theatrical creation.
Yet in many subtle conjunctive coercions,
I have arrived in an ocean of confusion.
Why did I not resist such a power?
Have my eyes been glued and my tongue made mute?
How did I arrive at this destination of nothingness?
It began with attraction, which transformed into lust,
then converted to passion,
followed by courtship,
commitment,
excitement,

confusion,
disagreement,
depression.
Drowning each other in petty, bullet-point arguments,
subjecting each other to a miserable existence—
What sort of life is this?
This is not living,
but rather imminent procrastinated death.
They are seeds of doom, radical in growth—
poison mixed with selfish pleasure.
We were picture perfect,
beautiful and abundant in love, but I became your serpent
and you my forbidden fruit. So where does that leave us?

THE LITTLE GREEN GIRL

Last night I had a dream of a lady in green.
She was a flower—
man was she a beautiful scene—
she had the brightness of the sun behind her.
Yes, she is my angel,
and
yes, I testify that love's pain is a danger,
but to this forbidden flower,
I surrender my love unconditional every hour,
as I bit into this fruit to let the passion unleash
I started getting deeper and found all her secrets released.
As time went by, she and I were stuck like glue.
I gotta be real, I had my doubts. I wasn't always optimistic,
but I knew my love was true—
she wasn't going to play me like a fool,
and then it hit me like something ballistic—
consciousness took over as I rose from the unrealistic.
Seasons changed, and my lady green changed color—
she was no longer my flower.

———————————————

FRIENDSHIP & FORGIVENESS

I forgive you, my friend.
I wish you peace.
If you wonder why I stand afar
It's because this wound that I carry has left a scar.
Our interaction is done—
time for me to heal,
time to confront my pain and shed my fear,
raining these tears held in here.
Old friend,
what hurt you must have to create such storms—
conflict like thunder,
shocking words.
What you carry inside, you have shared with me.
Now I have a glimpse of the lens through which you see.
I hope to understand and empathize with your plea.
In this spark of fire,
it is easy to be angry and very easy to hate—
I shall continue to build strength to show you kindness,
letting go of ignorance and blindness,
reaching out to create peace for me and for you.

OVERCOME

Every day is a new opportunity,
to work smarter,
push harder,
to outdo me.

———————

GOOD MORNING

Consciousness settles into this body.

Gathering self out of the scattered arena of sleep.
Thoughts come and go.
Decisions start to be made.
Aversion to rise is obvious.
Attachment to sleep is dominant.
Time draws near the moment of departure.
The motivator is overwhelming.
I notice how I use my thoughts
to propel this body upward.
I realize more now
that my whole existence is mind.
Sensations
drawing the outside world into mind
for interpretation.
The familiar, the unfamiliar,
those connected to memory,
those creating memories and back to decisions,
followed by action.

———————————

PEACE

A sigh of relief,
exhaling the heaviness of the week,
exhaling the smog of stressors that at times surround me,
exhaling disappointments and stringent expectations,
loneliness and dissatisfaction,
coughing out anxiety and toxic tensions.
Inhale the freshness of peace,
inhale love that hugs a hurt heart,
inhale gentleness,
inhale kindness,
inhale words that soothe the pains of the soul,
inhale generosity that fills an empty bowl.

OBSTACLE

Life is full of obstacles—
we must not succumb to them,
but rather exercise our power to overcome them
time and time again.
It is not a luxury but a necessity.
Just as we have overcome the obstacle of
crossing rivers by creating the bridge,
overcome the obstacle of
transportation by creating the wheelbarrow,
carriage,
bicycle,
car and the airplane.
We invented mail and the internet
to overcome the time it takes to communicate,
and shelter to shield us from the elements.
We all have the ability to overcome
our personal and social struggles.
It is easy to imagine the solution as arriving effortlessly.
Infrequently that might be true,
but very frequently, it is the opposite.

To surpass the challenge of an obstacle, one may begin with rudimentary and elementary methods.

It may involve a process of trial and error, failure and the recognition and acquisition of knowledge from the failure to do once more until the intended goal is accomplished.

In other words, we may find obstacles within obstacles.

It is a journey whose outcome might not be as we plan or imagine, but nonetheless, a journey worth taking for the progress of our family, friends, community, environment and ourselves. It is a noble undertaking that drives our evolution.

It is our birthright.

———————————

LIFE

The sweet sound of morning awakens my soul,
life's cycle endlessly unfolds,
eternally pushing this boulder uphill,
flowing melodies massaging anguish,
ancestral pangs traversed through history and time,
locked in this earthly being.
A bright sun fades from mysterious forests.
Despite it all,
I have danced with the winds,
burned with fire,
tended seeds into fruit-bearing trees,
flew too high with wings of wax.
Volcanic eruption settled the ashes of anger.
I have loved like the swan.
Winter silence befalls my soul into frost.

DARE

Dare to create.
Dare to be bold.
Dare to inspire.
Dare to be inspired.
Dare to be fearless,
Courageous.
Dare to go where others won't go,
see what others don't see,
to reveal what's in here out there.
Dare to be curious.
Dare to share.

———————

THE VOICE INSIDE

Young brother, keep your head up.
The struggle has just begun, so don't give up.
Be proud, and dry your tears from your eyes.
Young sister, walk tall.
You will fall sometimes, but just get up and walk tall.
Life ain't easy,
surviving is a chance we take.
Believe me,
success is a process we sometimes eliminate
because at times,
it's a long process filled with multiple mistakes.
Young brother, keep your head up.
This ain't the place for you.
Don't be a caged bird singing beautiful
songs for no one to hear.
Share with the world songs from your wandering heart.

WINNING RECIPE

Tired,
searching,
frustrated.
The answer,
does it exist?
Stretched,
angry,
hungry.
The larger the fight,
the larger the courage that is required in a woman
or man.
Lost,
focused,
determined.
Every ounce of me is being given.
Driven,
afraid,
misguided.
The road never ends,
the growth never ends, it never, ever, ends.
Motivated, accepting, confused.

The pressure rises beyond my thermal gauge.
Vulnerable, tired. Pacing and enduring this distance race.
Winning.
Every progress is a win.
Every lesson learned is a victory.
This is life,
the beautiful green grass beyond the darkness of failing.
In the face of adversity,
where there is much to lose in pursuit of one's dreams,
there is much to gain.
Rise out of the trenches of self-doubt, and
break the chains of timidity over and over again.
Be a bright star in the night guiding others
looking for a way.

SEEING AND KNOWING

Let's not let the celebration of tradition be the
only time we practice giving. Give every day.
Give kind words,
kind actions,
your time.
Give, expecting nothing in return.

COMPOSITION OF DEATH

Death I spoke as my last breath fled my body,
ashes to ashes—
as words through my optic passes as I lived,
ashes to ashes,
to bones as skin decomposes,
a body without spirit—
as spirits mourning a soul,
who will follow my footsteps and mistakes correct,
to correct the human imperfect defect?

_____

MATTER

Spawn of this material world,
eating matter,
excreting matter,
loving matter.
What does it matter?

TIME

My enemy has agility and unconditional stamina.
She is the beauty that brings butterflies to my stomach
and weakens my knees.
He is and always will be a leader
and I a follower.
My enemy is time—
time past,
time present,
time yet to come—
a time to wake,
a time to lie,
a time to eat,
a time for work and a time for play.
Even the moment of thought,
to this paper is somehow relative to time.
Time is always forward-moving.
With time I grow older and stronger,
soon old and weak.
Time is a fierce yet beautiful enemy,
a dangerous and constantly progressing entity.
What a penalty it is to go before your time,
but we must not fear it.

SCHOOL IS OUT

It's time to say goodbye,
as this day passes
at last, it's time to say goodbye,
friends and foes go home,
teachers,
students,
together,
alone.
All in one building,
but not all problems known,
shown—
goodbye we say at last,
farewell,
farewell to the past.

_____

THE STRUGGLE

Life's cause,
what loss,
mistakes I make to expand my brain—
imperfections have lessons,
as students have questions.
Books and chapters have answers,
whereas life is a cancer,
spreading and unstable,
weak and unable is a mind drowning in depression.
To concentrate and elevate above negativity
leaves an impression and shows strength.

HOME SWEET HOME

I closed my eyes, and I drifted away,
thinking of the warmth of the West African sun,
kissing the surface of my skin.
Home sweet home.
Now a mirage in my thoughts, evaporates,
but never lost in my heart where it lies.
Eyes closed, and Mother Africa calling my name,
my spirit,
my soul.
I awake, crying for my home sweet home.

REALIZE

My fist,
my heart and soul channeled through a punch.
Anger,
frustration,
released through the air
with the pounding echo of my fist making contact.
I fear
so I punch before I can understand.
I am a reflex of my own emotions.
You kick me.
I kick back.
You insult me, I return the same.
I have no control of me, the reflex.
I act now to think later—
that is the negative.
I control my reflex, and when overwhelmed, I deny or
reject this reflex.
All control is mine.
Before I move,
I think.
Before I speak, even before I wake.
I am no longer a reflex—
the reflex is only part of who I am.

LAZY BOY

This old chair,
stained,
ripped,
deflated,
waiting in open embrace,
ready to serve another sit.

——————————————

BREATH

Peace comes from within.
To know this peace,
one must learn to be still,
silent,
and comfortable in this place.

MOON

My joy will not fade with the sunset,
for the moon has a smile just as bright.
I look forward to seeing her,
her fair complexion,
her round glow and radiant aura—
she lights up my world.
She is a silent beauty,
distant and mysterious,
cautiously floating across the heavens.
With each passing day, she reveals a different expression—
she surrounds me with love,
teasing me carefully with her play,
appearing in the dark and vanishing in the day.

DON'T PLAY WITH FIRE

I dance around the fire burning,
flaming,
biting each hair on skin,
melting,
draining life out of boiling veins,
sparking nerves,
exploding signals to mind,
ash sinking to the sand,
hand,
palm sweating,
hurting,
fire burning,
flickering with the wind,
uncertain which way it blows,
uncertain which way it blows.

METAMORPHOSIS

Magnificent hibiscus
with the sun's presence in every raw leaf.
Dew sliding down,
falling helplessly to the dry sand—
each curve and sweet scent allures with a satisfying,
arousing potency.
Rain allows the history on the surface
to sink deeper into the soil.
The decaying leaf,
the footstep,
the lifeless,
nourishing and sinking deeper.
With the invisible exchange of carbon dioxide and oxygen,
I am one with the hibiscus.
Imagining that every exhale with its length,
Speed, and force
reveals valuable unconscious intelligence to hibiscus
and thus, I too am on the receiving end of this influence.
It is a dance of sorts
that marks our initiation on this planet—
into this world—
and its extended cessation stands to mean
our departure and transformation.

MAY

May the winds blow my way,
carrying sadness far, far away,
bringing new light to my life and fresh air to stay.
As the sun sets,
I admire its orange glow,
leaving me speechless
as the warmth makes free my blood flow.
May the wind blow my way
never for my naked eyes to see,
yet to have its presence felt.
Oh, how powerful this wind is,
for it has large trees and fields of grass
swaying from left to right,
yet gentle, it befriends everyone
and knows us all inside and out.

———————————————

THE TIDE

The tides are rolling into the bay,
slapping and splashing against the rocks.
The tides are rolling into the bay,
pulling in and pushing out the sand.
Something special is happening today—
on the horizon, the sun gradually fades,
the cool breeze persuades the grass to dance,
the fish of the sea jump above the surface,
wishing for wings,
the colorful birds sing,
white clouds float by
morphing into and out of the familiar.
The tides are rolling into the bay,
sweeping in pieces of shipwrecked pasts,
tales of love,
bottles of rum,
sweat and tears for treasures that have sunk,
villains,
sheroes
and heroes unsung.
The tide has rolled in, and it is floating out to sea,
taking with it a piece of me.

SPRING

Amazing grace,
what a beautiful day,
the sun is out, and things are going my way.
Amazing grace, not in a dramatic way,
not gray, all green and everything is simply gay.
The birds are singing—how sweet their song.
The flowers are blossoming—how sweet they smell.
I will cling to you, spring, as the seasons change.
I will dwell in this weather as if it will end never.

ROOTS

Every morning and through the passing day,
I see you.
Many pass by me, and with a single glance
they fall in a seductive trance,
wanting to touch and smell.
Dreaming of smooth soft petals
gently tickling one's skin.
Yet you pass me by daily
with your exterior blinding my eyes
and your presence filling me with warmth.
Unlike the others, you never notice me.
I feel so close to you yet so far away.
At times
I see your sadness consume you with dark clouds,
making you no longer visible to the world;
I wait patiently
as your tears drown my roots with hope.

I await another passing,
another glance of you smiling
and the feeling of your warm touch on my face.
I love you,
my sun and golden star.
Yours truly,
Rose.

———

LOVE

When people understand true love,
self-love,
reciprocity is second nature.

FEELINGS

My heart has its own signature beat to the thought of you.
Couldn't imagine myself feeling this again,
yet here I am. Who knew?
Listening to the rhythm of my heart
and filtering it through logic and analysis,
trying to compute years of conditioning and biases,
With every interaction, more of me keeps unraveling
like a lotus slowly opening.
Despite curiosity, I still question whether this is reality,
going with the flow and taking each step carefully,
serendipity, a coincidental genesis,
trying not to make too much of this.
No expectations, no illusions,
I want to do what's right by you.
If you need support—a friend—I'm here—
here to be what you need, not what I want.

IN PLAIN SIGHT

Every time I see you my heart beats faster,
my smile is wider—
you are my natural high—
there might even be a twinkle in my eyes.
For a second all my worries are set aside.
I enjoy the color of your hair,
the sound of your voice,
the warmth of your presence,
longing for more of you in your absence.
You are a well-written poem,
a captivating story,
a cool drink, and shade beneath a desert sun.
You are fun and adventurous,
smart and vivacious—
your beauty is outrageous.
You are a melody. I shall forever be enchanted by thee.

REFLECTION

I have been so busy surviving,
distracting myself from life,
that on occasion when I get to stop,
I realize how much I have been missing—
colorful flowers blossoming outside my window,
the still trees and the singing birds,
the endless sky,
the traveling of noise through silence.
I notice myself.
The journey traveled through time asleep
and now temporarily awakened—
what a beautiful feeling,
so outstanding.
It's unfortunate because at times,
I see myself as just another contestant
running in this human race.

At times,
I struggle to calm these thoughts clashing with reality
like ocean waves against rocks.
Bouncing in and out of consciousness.
Awake,
aware
but dreaming.
Regardless of this inconsistency,
I pull myself back to the beauty beyond my window
and the beauty within myself to find peace
once again and again and again.

———————————————

LOVE

I want to be in love again'
I want that romance that excites me for the sake of being.
I want to be happy.
I want to be in unison with another being
in a fluid, intrinsic way.
I want to share this deep love of life and of me.
I want reciprocity and cooperation,
understanding and teamwork.
I want someone who can speak, understand and navigate
my mental and emotional language, and vice versa.
I want peace as clear as a breath of fresh air.
I want compatibility so good that it's almost nearly perfect,
at least for me.
I want a healthy, positive and enriching relationship
with a solid, strong foundation.
I want communication so in tune that it seems telepathic.
I want it all,
but in order to find the love that I want,
I must first find and love myself.

LOVING THEE

I love you as a human being, clearly unconditionally.
I love you compassionately, respectfully and carefully.
I love you strongly,
often mighty intensely.
I love you imperfectly,
honestly and questionably.
I love you frequently,
occasionally, sadly,
loving immaturely,
immensely, tumultuously.
I love you proudly.
Oh, so proudly.
I love you generously,
infinitely,

timely,
impatiently,
uncertainly,
spontaneously,
mysteriously,
unbelievably.
Who knew it could be—
a love like you and me.
I love you forgivingly,
continuously, endlessly,
continuously, endlessly,
continuously, endlessly.

_____

SUNSET

Let's walk together
till our time expires,
till the moon and the sun are in awe of our love.
Be loving so the sun may admire and imitate your shine.
Let us walk together
and talk about this experience called life,
for it has us brought us pain and joy,
separation and togetherness.
Let us not forget our love for each other.
May it never fade with age,
for the gift of love from the creator—
we will try to share with everyone.

WHAT TO MAKE OF LOVE

Is love to be what one's eyes see and lust to feel,
feeling your heart pound furiously as if looking for escape
from your chest,
and every breath says, love.
The mind drifts out of curiosity,
drowning in lustful passion or romance.
Is love to be what others' thoughts disagree?

LOVE CURES

Enjoy life, for you only live once,
it can easily slip away.
Don't be afraid to tell the people you care about that
you love them, or show them with a really nice hug.
Show kindness to people whether you know them or not—
simply open a door or say thank you.
Smile more often.
It might seem absurd, but it actually
helps one feel better.
Be positive and forgive yourself.
Love cures.

———————

FIRE

Obstacles are there to be overcome,
to help us realize how truly special we are.
They are there to help us understand our strengths
and never surrender to our weaknesses.

HEARTS AND MINDS

We are a band of brothers thrown into unfortunate circumstances, and some will not make it out of here alive. That is a reality we all live with. Our last mission took the life of Doc. You see, Doc was a good man, a family man. His children were his pride and joy, and that's all he talked about. He always wore a smile, and every once in a while, he would show the boys a picture of his old lady. She was quite a looker.

When he spoke of how good she was to him, I heard paradise in his voice and saw heaven in his eyes. He took care of all of us like we were his children. All the men in Alpha Squad respected the Doc. We knew that in the heat of battle, if we got hit, the Doc would be there to patch us right up—he was known for it. He was caught in the crosshairs of a sniper's scope, and a bullet to the face ended his life. The squad has never been the same.

There came to be an unspoken emptiness in us. We saw our Doc die. A few days later, a new guy was assigned as Doc's replacement. That is the beauty of war; there is no time to mourn. The moment one sets foot on the field of battle, each experience is a tearing of weaknesses and a building of hardened calluses. Out here, even if we do cry, it's a bitterness that only drips on the inside. Angel was the name of the new guy, but the guys called him Darkie. He was a tall, big and dark negro.

I was never fond of the idea of them sending a negro to do a man's job. Every morning he would wake up with his boots filled with sand, and his uniform would smell like piss. Yet like an angel, he never got bent out of shape. He knew what he was in for, being the black sheep. We all hated this man and wanted him gone, but it was all too late. Alpha Squad got assigned a mission, and this included Darkie.

We all knew this was the moment he was waiting for. His time had come, and if one of us got hit, we knew we were dead men. As we walked down the dirt road to the rendezvous point, oddly, I began to feel a sense of calm, and my mind wandered in the thought of life back home— imagining what people might be up to.

Here I am, a man on a mission, a soldier in a war, and I want to win without the blood of the enemy on my hands. How can this be over without death on my conscience?

I am an expert with this bayonet and quite proficient with my gun. I look to the silent sky, light blue and playful with the sun displaying its beauty and ever stretching brightness. I have never witnessed sailing clouds so peaceful in their pace and yet so animated. Why must something so ugly happen under this magnificent sky? I hear the hissing sound of dry leaves in dancing trees being blown by the wind—beautiful.

Our sacrifice for this country is not voluntary, but we must, so we do it for those we love. We have all made it our duty to make sure each man returns to his family. Each step we take ages me. Our mission is to engage the enemy in a small town, twenty klicks north-east of our location. As we approach the town, each man wears his battle face fueled by angst, anger and sexual deprivation.

If only I knew a way to prevent my mind from preserving memories of what we will witness. We heard guns blasting, and the fight began. Nothing could have prepared me for this: "Feet don't fail me now," I think as my heart races toward a finish unknown. I hear screams as bullets whistle past my head. My hands begin to shake. I am not very lucky; I am one of the first in the line of fire and one of the first to get hit.

The bullet fires directly into the side of my stomach, weakening me to the ground. As I lie there, experiencing mind-arresting pain, I scream and scream and scream. It was no choice of mine to be in this war. Darkie rushed to me with urgent speed, and as he pulled out his field knife, I knew I was dead for sure, but quickly, he slid the sharp edge across the front of my shirt and ripped it open. He was quick. He kept me stable and began to inspect the wound without uttering a single syllable.

His great big arms controlled my body as if I were a puppet. He quickly wrapped my whole middle section with bandages to slow the bleeding, and this gave me hope.

"It's a flesh wound soldier, a flesh wound."

It all happened so fast, and in the speed of light, he was gone, tending to the wounds and cries of the next man. He was precisely the man we needed, and from that day onward, he became the Doc, our Doc. We realized we had an Angel for a doc—a mild-mannered man who was an expert at his job. He was a family man, but he didn't speak much about them. He was a very good listener. We all became very fond of the Doc and showed him great respect. I thought about all the things we did and said to him when he first arrived. I felt very ashamed and apologetic, but my pride always kept me from saying I was sorry.

TWIST A & E

After a long deep slumber, Adam woke up to a marvelous, wondrous sight. "Wow," he said. "God, this is the most amazing creature you have ever made. I have to say that this is your best work." Every curve on her body was perfect, and as he watched in amazement, lost in her brown eyes, black hair, and beautiful brown skin, he felt himself being pulled closer and closer to her. His loneliness was no more, for now he had found the one who completes his heart. Adam could not wait to show her all of Eden, and she was also thrilled to be with him. As Adam showed her around, he taught her about all the things that God made and their names. Adam realized she was a fast learner, much faster than he, and he loved her for that. Eve quickly learned all about Eden; she tasted every fruit and climbed every tree. She knew every space and corner of Eden even better than Adam, but it seemed to her that something was missing, and when she told Adam, he mentioned to her that he knew exactly how she felt. One bright, perfect afternoon, with grass a perfect green, with flowers a perfect sweet smell, Adam saw that it was time for Eve to know God's rule about their future in Eden.

"Eve," he called.

"Yes, Adam," she replied.

"It is God's plan that you and I populate this earth with our offspring, but we must wait until he tells us to. If we begin before he instructs us, then we shall fall out of his favor, and we will die." Eve now knew what was missing, and from the moment Adam told her, she could not stop her curious eyes from admiring every rock-hard muscle on Adam's smooth pale skin. She could not help herself. Each word he spoke made her fall deeper and deeper into a trance called Adam. He was the apple of her eye, and she wanted to taste every bit of it. Eve tried to distract herself, but she could not. A voice in her head kept confirming and inflaming her desire. Over time these emotions grew stronger, not only in Eve, but also in Adam. It had now been six days since the birth of Eve. God spoke to them that day, and they realized how pleased God was with them for being patient and loving with each other.

After God was done with them, it was dark, so Adam and Even decided to take a bath in a hot spring before going to sleep. They sat opposite each other, and as they looked into each other's eyes, their emotions grew stronger. They began to inch forward toward one another, and as their bodies met and their lips touched in the middle of the steaming hot spring, there was no going back. Every single lustful thought was acted out, and so it seems that Adam and Even had now disobeyed God and started far too soon.

The next morning came, and Adam and Eve were still asleep in each other's arms. Afternoon came, and they were at it again, immersed in lustful passion until moments later, God came and saw them. They witnessed God's fury as the perfect sky darkened, and lightning began to strike. "Adam!" called God.

"Yes, Father," he replied.

"You have disobeyed me, and so have you Eve, my daughter. You have acted against my instructions, and so my beloved daughter and son, you will face this world without me to directly guide you. You two have grown out of my rules; therefore you have grown out of the home I have made for you."

From that moment on, it was out of the garden for Adam and Eve and into the harsh world. They began to face many adversities they were not familiar with, but with time they learned to adapt.

Eventually, Adam and Eve learned to do things like gathering food and building shelter. The two had an unbreakable bond and great love for each other, but they did not always agree and had moments where one could not bear the sight of the other. There was one instance

where Adam got angry and told Eve that she was too
demanding. Yelling at the sky he said,
"I want to sail the curves of her ocean
and dive into the depth of her heart.
I want to capture every moment—prolong—but the
fragrance of this flower is temporary.
Free me from this belligerent evil.
Ghosts escape my throat, striking fear in your soul.
Do you seek my demise?
For at times, it is you I despise.
Don't cry butterfly.
Preying on my weakness, you smell regret in my sighs.
You defuse the anger in my bloodshot eyes,
so I fall for the bait—
I drop the weight of bewildering hate,
and there,
you escape the terror which was to be your fate.
Oh, this beautiful butterfly.
My eyes are fixed on her as she floats to the sky,
her array of colors has my eyes hypnotized.
I want to sail the curves of her ocean
and dive into the depth of her heart.
I want to capture every moment—prolong—but her
sweetness is poison
slithering her venom into my veins, and my mind bemuse
Rescue me—
I am her puppet.
She pulls my strings

my sanity is now a mere internal debate."
Arguments and disagreement between the two were
common, but they always managed to talk through
challenges and continued loving one another. When Adam
felt angry, he at times felt so emotional he would express it
by breaking or throwing things. On the other hand, when
Eve was angered, her words could be piercing, methodical
and sometimes vicious, shooting directly into Adam's
heart to spread to the veins in order to subdue the angry
beast Adam would become. They were not living a perfect
life, but what always seemed perfect and always alive was
the bond that began in the Garden of Eden. Adam and
Eve had offspring—twins—and this caused them to grow
closer together as a family. The boy was called Joseph and
the girl was Mary. Their parents taught them everything
they knew of the world. They taught their children about
God and the history of the garden of Eden. Mary grew to
become a humble, gentle, respectful woman, but Joseph
was the complete opposite. He was stubborn and filled
with pride. He blamed his parents for each day of hardship
they faced and was always dwelling on what would have
happened if they had not disobeyed God. Adam is now
an old man, who takes delight in the simple things in life
such as marveling at high landscapes, watching the sunset
or gathering everyone around a fire and telling stories of
times past. Yet Adam and Eve's love was not enough
to calm Joseph's rage against them. The two men grew
further and further apart. Joseph saw Adam as unfit to lead

the family and tried to convince Mary to run away with him to begin a new life, but she declined and convinced him to stay.

Joseph decided that if he were to stay, then he must be the leading male in the family, no matter the cost. That night Joseph called on his father to go with him alone to watch the sunset. It was a particularly cold night, and the sunset was especially marvelous, appearing to last longer than usual. Adam stood up, walked to the edge of the mountain, and admired the far hilltops and flowing rivers. He took a deep breath and patiently exhaled. He turned to Joseph and said, "Come and embrace me my son. Today I will go home a happy man." Joseph embraced his father, and with the swiftness of a snake, drove a dagger into his back. With tears in his eyes, Adam uttered in his dying breath, "Death I spoke as my last breath fled my body, ashes to ashes—
as words through my optic passes as I lived, ashes to ashes, to bones as skin decomposes, a body without spirit—
as spirits mourning a soul, who will follow my footsteps and mistakes correct, to correct the human imperfect defect?"

When Joseph returned, Mary and Eve were sitting around a fire talking, bonding, and laughing, but they were startled when they saw Joseph. There was blood on his hands and clothes. "What happened, Son?" asked Eve as she rushed to Joseph. "Where is your father!" With tears in her eyes, she demanded again, screaming, "Where is he!"

As Joseph stood there motionless with his face bowed toward the ground, Mary knew what Joseph had done. "Father is dead."

Six days passed after the death of Adam, and Eve was broken-hearted, alone. She did not eat, nor did she drink. Eventually she stopped going outside of her hut all together. Mary went into her mother's living quarters to mourn with her and comfort her. When Mary saw her mother, she was sitting down with a cup in hand, crying. "Please, please say it ain't so.

Tears sprint out of my eyes and swim down my cheeks.
Say it ain't so.
He was my best friend,
So this is my reality.
I pinch myself to escape and awake from this darkness.
I am screaming inside, but no one hears my voice.
Memories have become my enemy,
so I get angry at GOD and everyone around me.
I beg, and I cry—suddenly I believe in miracles.
I wait impatiently for mine, for a sign.
This helpless emotion is my new addiction.
This pain has injured my feeble body—
the magnitude, the burden—
cursing at the heavens as the weight forces me down on my

knees.

My sunshine is gloom.

My heart only sees doom.

One tip of this cup and the grim sight of lifeless flesh in a tomb—

life has wounded my heart.

Life has scrambled my sanity.

The wind has blown the fire from this melting candle.

I Will Rest. In. Peace."

———————————

THE GAME

September 23rd, 2012. I woke up to a chilly Sunday morning. The time was 8:30 a.m. My boyfriend invited me to watch one of his Sunday morning soccer games that he was so religious about. This is a man who is well known for oversleeping during important appointments and showing up tardy to work. Yet on Sundays, he is quite punctual for "football" as he so calls it.

I was lying on the bed, on my left side with the sun's rays seeping through the blinds warmly against my skin. Then as I was about to find my way out of the rabbit hole, this five-foot-eight-inch Ghanaian man wakes me with a stern and loving shake. "Babe, babe, babe."
I opened my eyes slowly, rolled on my back, stretching out of the comfortable fetal position I was in and uttered the words, "Okay, I'm up, I'm up. Soccer, right?"
Getting a whiff of my morning breath, he quickly stepped back and said, "Babe, brush your teeth, and yes, soccer."

I laughed a bit on the inside. "I will be out in the car," he said. "Breakfast is on the table." Knowing how much this means to him, I hurriedly waddled my way around and got ready. The drive to the soccer field was short—relatively five minutes driving time. It was a quiet ride. I was still gradually regaining consciousness, and he was focused, preparing himself mentally for the game ahead.

When we arrived, everyone was already there. The time was 9 a.m. The sun was shining bright, the field was almost perfectly trimmed with lines visibly drawn from goal post to goal post. It seemed I was the only spectator for the day. I watched carefully and attentively, fascinated by the friendly and playful way they bonded. I stood and hovered over the short fence close to James's teams' goal post and also next to the parking lot.

There were various ages, genders, and cultures on the field. Each wearing the jersey of a team or player they admire. I saw the blue and white Chelsea jersey, the red and blue Barcelona, the black and white Ghana jersey, the blue France jersey, and many others. Most players were wearing cleats, and others had on sneakers. One thing James mentioned to me some time ago was that you could almost always identify the newbie—the person just starting to learn how to play.

In most cases, in a pickup game, it's the person with the neatest jersey, wearing fully color-coordinated gear. Sure enough, he was correct. There he was—a young boy who looked to be about fifteen and with blue cleats, black socks covering his shin guards, with a blue Italian jersey, and the name of the Italian national teams' goalkeeper and captain "Buffon" on the back. This boy moved with very poor coordination, allowing the ball to control him like a puppet. It was quite a comical sight. Then, at last, the game began, and the whole mood changed.

It was reds vs. blues. Each went into position ready for battle, and battle they did. There was yelling, shoving, sliding tackles, bicycle kicks, and marvelous, wind-bending goals. I was enjoying it so much I completely forgot how cold it was outside. The time was 11:25 a.m., and the game was nearing its end. The score was red 8, blue 9. They agreed that if blue scored one more goal, the game would be over, but if red scored, they would keep playing for a final point.

These things are never decided in the beginning of the pickup games. Normally, they play their hearts out first and then randomly decide how it will end based on the score. James was on the blue team this time—man of the match, putting away the most goals and assists. I was so proud of him. Typically, James is the pacifist, naturally resolving conflicts and leading in his own way. This time he was the commander on the field of battle, shouting coordinates and keeping the team running.

Then it happened, right when red least expected. A pass from midfield to Marta, the forward right striker, a header, the keeper diving and touching it with his fingertips; but it was not enough, and there it was—the finishing goal. There were ecstatic screams and jubilant celebrations of the goal. The blue team was quite happy to say the least. Each player was walking around with a large grin. Surprisingly, the red team was not upset either. They all went back to being their jolly selves—students, doctors, cooks, computer techs—all now going their separate ways. Daughters, uncles, mothers, and fathers moving on to play their different roles in life—until next Sunday.

_____

AMUN

In the face of adversity,
where there is much to lose in the pursuit of one's
dreams,
there is much to gain.
Rise out of the trenches of self-doubt,
and break the chains of timidity over and
over again.
Be a bright star in the night for
others looking for a way.

———————————

Greatness is born every day.
Unfortunately, it is not always uncovered.
However, when the moment arrives
and the battle within self is won,
the revelation is magical.

You have so much beauty in you.
Don't lose sight of it due to the ignorance of another.

You are precious, but at times, in order to see it,
one must work,
digging deep within to arrive at the truth,
the beautiful truth.

If you hold on to the hurt,
all you will feel is pain.
Letting go can be challenging.
It takes repeated work.
You might feel vulnerable in the process.
That's part of it.
Do the work and be happy.

Love is within you,
and you must share it with the world.
If you are searching for love,
look no further than yourself.

Happiness is making all that you are and all that you do an extension of love.

I am learning how to be of service to humanity.
I don't really know why I am here, but while here if I can
make a positive difference in one person's life, then great.
If many people, even better.
Hopefully, it's a lasting effect.
If not, at least for a time, that person has some peace,
experiencing kindness and love.
I don't know what the future holds.
We aren't guaranteed the next second, let alone a month or
a year.
All we can do is make the best of this moment, whatever
the best is at this time.

Mothers make the world go 'round,
and we honor you today and every day.
With gratitude and compassion, thank you.